Stürtz REGIO

SPREE FOREST

Text by
Volker Oesterreich

Photos by
Hans-Rudolf Uthoff

SPREEWALD

Ahrensdorf

179

96 Teupitz Halbe

Baruth 13 Unterspreewald

Schlepzig

Charlotten-
felde 115 Golssen Spree

Lübben 8 Biosphäre

102 Dahme Luckau **Lübbenau** 3 5 Leh

87 Raddusch

Hohenbucko Niede

96 Calau

**Finster-
walde**

13

1 Bahnhof Burg
(Spreewald-Spezialitätenrestaurant)

2 Aussichtspunkte für den
Braunkohletagebau

3 Haus für Mensch und Natur
(Biosphärenreservat-Ausstellung)

4 Naturschutzgebiet Hochwald

5 Naturlehrpfad Lübbenau - Lehde

6 Schinkel-Kirche

7 Schloss und Park Branitz

8 Mittelalterlicher Wehrturm

9 Spreewaldmuseum

10 Jugendstiltheater

Stürtz REGIO

SPREE FOREST

Text by
Volker Oesterreich

Photos by
Hans-Rudolf Uthoff

Front cover top: Fliessen-landscape near Raddusch. Cover centre: signboard at the Lübbenau barge harbour. Cover bottom: front-door, traditional Sorbian gowns. Back cover: Jutta Pudenz, the Spree Forest postwoman, delivering mail.

Pages 4/5: the former Spree Forest train station in Burg has been lovingly restored. Today it houses a restaurant which offers Spree Forest specialities.

Pages 8/9: in the midst of fern and Fliessen this lonely house in Burg conveys a wonderful sense of calm. The driveway has been replaced by a landing-place for barges.

The Authors:

Volker Oesterreich is the arts and culture editor of the Berliner Morgenpost and lives in Berlin.

Hans-Rudolf Uthoff is a free-lance photographer in Hamburg.

Credits

Photos:
Archiv für Kunst und Geschichte, Berlin:
p. 26 bottom left; p. 60 top right.
Rainer Weisflog, Cottbus: p. 40-41

Die Deutsche Bibliothek - CIP catalogue record
Spree Forest / Hans-Rudolf Uthoff (photographer),
Volker Oesterreich (author). –
Würzburg: Stürtz 1998.
ISBN 3-8003-1062-7 / paperback

Approved licence issue for
Verlagshaus Würzburg GmbH & Co. KG,
Würzburg, Germany, 2002

© 1998 Stürtz Verlag, Würzburg, Germany

Design: Förster Illustration & Grafik, Rimpar
Cartography: Steffen Oberländer, Munich
Repro: Atelier Hofmüller, Linz
Translation: Mélisa Dangel, Augsburg
Printed and processed by the
by the Offizin Andersen Nexö Leipzig

ISBN 3-8003-1062-7 / paperback

CONTENTS

ON THE FLIESSEN DREAMS AND REALITY CONVERGE

In the Spree Forest everything is different: when you put all your eggs in one basket, it doesn't mean that you risk losing all your valuables but rather that you are using a masterpiece of local craftsmanship to hold them. A farmer plodding through the wet marshland in his slippers has not forgotten to put on his proper shoes – he is merely protecting his feet with the locally popular wooden clogs, which are still manufactured according to old design. And when a bride steps before the marriage altar in traditional Spree Forest attire (unfortunately no longer a common practice), she is dressed entirely in black.

Once arrived in Lehde, you can enjoy the cheerful coming and going of visitors exploring the region on foot and in barges.

Another curiosity of the Spree Forest is to be found in ship building: boats here are low and lie flat in the water. Otherwise the barges would run aground on the 340 miles of navigable waterways and canals, the so-called "Fliessen" (the complete system of Fliessen measures more than 620 miles in length). And nobody wants this to happen. Certainly not the two million visitors who season after season come to the southeast of Brandenburg to sit on rocking boats and admire the beauty of a water meadow landscape that is without comparison in Europe. And not the local farmers who use barges to transport their cattle to pasture or even ship light-weight farm engines to their vegetable

fields on two barges that have been tied together. To make this possible the barges are constructed in such a way that even with a minimal amount of water under their bellies they can still travel.

As flat as some Fliessen may be, the wooden bridges that cross them are especially high. These "Bänke", as they are known to the locals, allow the ferryman to remain standing as he passes under them. Whoever chooses to explore this predominantly flat region on foot, however, must be

Spree Forest – not least because she is frequently accompanied by television crews who attempt to bring a bit of spice to everyday working life in Germany. This may be a bother, but Jutta is good-natured about it. She would rather have the press board her barge than that of the fire brigade, who also depend on the customary wooden boats for some of their operations. When St. Florian, the patron saint of firemen, calls, an outboard engine may be employed. On most Fliessen this is strictly taboo.

A protective landmark: the city wall and Trutzer (left) date back to the 15th century. They are remnants of the ancient city ramparts. The Classicist Schloss Lübbenau lies in a landscape-park and today houses a hotel.

prepared to climb over plenty of bridge steps.

Another unusual feature here is the way the post is delivered. Everyone in Lehde knows the local postwoman, Jutta Pudenz. She punts through her postal district in a yellow barge and delivers the post to boxes that are mounted directly along the Fliessen. Jutta is a familiar sight in the

The Spree Forest people never had money to burn. Most farmers, craftsmen and fishermen barely made a living. Later on, the exploitation of lignite (brown coal) reserves in the peripheral areas temporarily led to an economic boom. In the meantime, most coal miners have lost their jobs. Today tourism remains the principle source of financial hope.

If you delve more deeply into the Spree Forest past,

you discover another branch of Spree economy which, alongside the once prosperous linen industry, brought some money into the area: "milk production" by wet nurses who were in high demand in the nearby cities of Berlin and Cottbus. Women from the countryside were considered especially healthy. Moreover, the people from the big cities believed that their offspring would imbibe the piety of Spree Forest wet nurses along with their milk. Quite a number of young mothers neglected their own children for the sake of this highly respected form of employment – employment to the detriment of the most defenceless members of society. But there were other reasons which forced many a young woman from the Spree Forest to become a wet nurse far from home. If she found herself pregnant before marriage, she was considered a woman of "ill-repute" – a deficiency for which she could make amends through her well-paid services.

Postal column near Lübbenau

The Spree Forest has often been compared to other famous regions, such as Venice, the Everglades in Florida or the Bayous in the Mississippi delta. These comparisons may seem far-fetched, but a closer look shows that the claims are not completely extravagant. After all, an organiser of cultural events once released a live alligator into the Fliessen in order to offer a musical open-air program with "bite"...

Fantasy has always been a trump card in this area.

People used to spend the long, dark winter nights telling each other tall tales such as the lore of the Wassermann or of the Sorb king's treasure, hidden away in the Schlossberg hill of Burg. But people also told stories of goblins and dragons or invented fabulous tales involving magical animals and daughters of water nymphs. The will-o'-the-wisp gave rise to particularly fantastic interpretations. For in those days, no one could explain the eerie glow that seemed to appear out of nowhere. Only today do we know that the strange light-phenomenon results from moor gases that

Straight as an arrow: a Fliess near Burg. The primary Spree reaches depths of 6 to 8 feet, whereas the other Fliessen are generally no more than 1.6 to 5 feet deep.

ignite during the night. Of all the mythical creatures and characters snakes have remained the most alive. The reptiles are found in the coat-of-arms of the Count of Lynar, who had the family emblem engraved in the wrought-iron gate of his Lübbenau castle; crossed snake-heads with crowns are also considered good luck symbols and often grace the gables of traditional Spree Forest homes. The most famous legend about snakes tells of the forester who cunningly filches the crown of the snake king, makes his get-away and soon becomes the owner of a large fortune. As legend has it, he is the founder of the Lynar dynasty.

According to elderly Spree Foresters, the extended labyrinth of waterways was also born from hair-raising circumstances. They believe the Devil himself had his fingers in the pie. One day, while plowing the fields, the Devil is said to have cursed so badly that the oxen broke loose and continued to run all over the place, with the plough steadily behind them. The plough, as the legend goes, dug the deep furrows through which the 300 Fliessen flow. In reality, the Fliessen bear witness to the Weichsel Ice Age. After the ice had planed the surface, the low incline of the land forced the river to fan out into many smaller side-arms and streams on its way through the rubble and alluvial sands that obstructed its original bed. As a result the 46 mile long and up to 10 mile broad lower and upper Spree valley emerged.

After the Spree Forest had been settled, the slight elevations between the Fliessen, the so-called "Kaupen", were used for agriculture and habitation. From the very

Traditional home-building: not only in Lehde, but also in places like Burg (pictured here) you can still find many of the traditional wooden Spree Forest houses.

beginning, the risk of floods or droughts required the Spree Foresters to stabilize the water level through additional canals, dams, and irrigation and drainage ditches. The first houses in

Despite such massive intrusions into nature and the large number of visitors, the Spree Forest remains

an El Dorado of rare fauna and flora.

A bisophere reserve spanning an area of 310 square miles, taken under the wings of UNESCO in 1990, is living proof of its natural diversity. During charabanc rides, guided hikes or canoe tours, the park rangers and guides barely manage to answer the many questions about the otter populations, the extremely rare black storks, the kingfisher birds or the glittering dragonflies. People

Lessons for city-slickers: the Buchenhain nature study path informs about the rich plant and animal life of the Lower Spree Forest.

the Spree Forest did not have cellars. A stone foundation at the highest point of the Kaupen supported the first layer of beams, so that the inhabitants rarely got their feet wet inside their log cabins. There were even "mobile homes" of a special kind: some houses were built on round logs and simply pulled a few feet higher upon safe ground whenever the water began to rise. Today an elaborate system of dammed-up lakes and drainage canals has greatly reduced the threat of floods.

even claim to have seen two pairs of sea-eagles, the German heraldic bird. But their breeding grounds are kept secret, so that these birds of prey which are threatened by extinction can be protected from poachers. At the heart of the reserve, restriction signs and sometimes even tree barriers prevent unwanted intruders from disturbing the nature refuge. One can only hope that the few incorrigible individuals who insist on venturing into the core area will be plagued by blood-sucking mosquito swarms; they, too, belong to the natural environment of the Spree Forest. Every idyll has its pitfalls.

Hiking, biking and canoeing

– these are the activities chosen by individualists. The majority of visitors, however, prefer to take things nice and slow: there are two-, four-, six-, and even eight-hour barge tours which have a wonderfully soothing effect on stressed-out city-dwellers. It is up to you to pick a tour of your liking. You can choose to visit the busy Upper Spree Forest or the hardly frequented Lower Spree Forest. You can arrange for a large outing with 30 other people or a private tour with your favorite friends. You can decide between your own picnic or a catered lunch, between a ferry-woman in traditional Sorbian Spree Forest attire or a ferryman in regular clothing. And there is always the difficult choice between either a dreamy mid-summer night tour in the moon light or a mid-day trip in the sweltering noon heat, under a canopy of leaves. There is a tour to suit everyone.

Whether you choose Burg, Raddusch, Vetschau, Lübbenau or Schlepzig as your point of departure, you can always count on finding a nearby harbour that offers informative, expertly-guided tours. In some of the smaller towns, you might arrive after all the boats have already left, but the towns of Burg, Lübbenau and Lübben almost always have space to offer on their barges. Even during especially busy weekends when streams of tourists descend on Lübben, the largest Spree Forest harbour, to savour the warm summer days with their picture-perfect skies, there is never remotely as much hustle and bustle as in the Frankfurt shopping district during summer sales. Once the ferryman has left the harbour and embarked on one of the many Spree side-arms, you are surrounded by heavenly peace.

Canoers in a sluice near Lehde

Except, of course, for the steady chirping and trilling of birds. Only in Lehde or in one of the traditional excursion spots will one find (what some people may think of as) highlife. But during the week there is hardly a trace of it.

During the week you can easily shift down a notch or two

and admire the dressed-up gardens of Spree Forest cabins while you drift along the alders, poplars, willow and birch trees that line the Fliessen. Both river banks occasionally feature the onion-shaped haystacks which are heaved onto wooden grids and prevent floods from ruining the crops. The outer layer protects from the rain the way a

only to bounce off the rippled surface of the Fliessen, scattering millions of light-reflections in all directions. At these moments, the visitor truly feels as if some magical creature has spoken "Open, Sesame!", allowing a glimpse of paradise. Dreams and reality converge on the Fliessen. Rude awakenings only occur to the individual canoer who suddenly finds himself lost without a water map of the Fliessen ...

Not only summer, but every season in the Spree Forest offers its attractions. In spring, the return of the migrant birds and the loud concerts of the frogs signal that nature is just about ready to "explode" with life energy. Autumn, on the other hand, enchants with its rich display of colours or melancholy landscapes, especially when

The harvested corn is being air-dried on a barn wall in Burg. Right: the Schinkel-Kirche of Straupitz, built in 1828, was recently restored at high expense. The large proportions of the church make it appear too big for the little town of Straupitz.

reet roof would. At times, the panorama is enhanced by unexpected sunrays which pierce through the canopy of leaves

clouds of fog waft through the evening twilight – atmospheric tableaux that no musical director could evoke on stage.

During winter the Fliessen are transformed into a paradise for ice-skaters. Again, one has to add, because only since the Lübbenau and Vetschau power stations were closed down in 1996 and heated cooling water is no longer channeled into the Spree Forest, has the Spree River begun to freeze over again in winter. Then the children of Leipe shoe their ice-skates and make their way to school in Burg, seven miles away, on the Fliessen. The *Lausitzer Rundschau* newsletter found this event worthy of a feature article, of course complete with photos of the hardy skaters. On weekends, when half of Berlin's ice-skating community flocks to the Spree Forest, the biting cold is easily forgotten amidst the fun and excitement. ■

As if it were a fortress of the pictorial arts: side view of the Cottbus Staatstheater.

Perhaps Liuba, the mythical goddess of love from Slavic legends, is hiding here? A birch-lined Fliess near Burg.

Previous double spread: you can only hope that she isn't delivering bills or prompt notices: Jutta Pudenz, the Spree Forest postwoman, at work in Lehde.

Impressions of Straupitz and Schlepzig: the Holländer mill has lost its blades. Today the mill not only grinds flour, but is also used for sawing and the production of flax oil (top). It is taken for granted that the storks, as shown here in Schlepzig, feel very much at home in the Spree Forest (centre). The migrant birds remain in the region from the beginning of April until the end of August.

The half-timbered church of
Schlepzig (bottom left and
right) has replaced a former
church building which burnt
down during a village fire.
The interior features a
fascinating blue ceiling,
at the centre of which the
symbolic eye of God has
been painted.

*Previous double spread:
the region of Schlepzig belongs to
the biosphere reserve that was listed
as a UNESCO protectorate at the
beginning of the 90s. In some parts
the jungle remains intact.*

The late Gothic Hallenkirche, built in 1607, stands right on the market square of Lübben. The church has three naves – a view of the interior (left) shows the altar and pulpit. The pastor and Baroque poet Paul Gerhardt held sermon in this church from 1669 until his death in 1676. The statue in front of the church tower was erected in his honour in 1907.

"DEPART, MY HEART, AND SEEK YE JOY ..."

The water-labyrinth at Raddusch might have inspired poets to literary heights.

In a region where myths and fairy tales thrive, it is not surprising that writers should also find literary inspiration. For example Theodor Fontane, whose travels to the Spree Forest in 1859 laid the foundation to his five-volume *Wanderings through the March of Brandenburg.* Fontane, the most Marchian of writers, caught the night–carriage down to the Spree Forest and explored

the "endlessly confusing river terrain"

for the newspaper *Preussischer Adler.* The three–day expedition not only prompted the poet to write some notes on the local cultivation of cucumbers, horse-radish and gourds but also challenged his journalistic talent – at least in one aspect. The Spree Forest costume of the women, which caught Fontane's attention during a Wendian or Sorbian mass, obviously proved too colourful for the poet to recreate for his readers in black and white print. The poet admitted that "to record in every detail its special nature is a task that I don't feel up to". He then, however, adds about

Writer Theodor Fontane began to take notes of his travels for the Wanderings in the Spree Forest.

twenty very detailed lines, as if he were trying to recommend himself as a fashion journalist.

But Fontane's literary musings really begin to flow once aboard one of the Spree Forest barges. Barely arrived in Lehde, he raves about the

"pocket-sized lagoon town".

There is "nothing lovelier to see" than this little town "that consists of as many islands as houses. The river forms the main street into which run narrow lanes from left and right." Today as then. The water path under its canopy of leaves even reminds the poet from Neu-ruppin of a poet's corner. Perhaps he found the right sentence rhythm

for his later great novels in the "rhythmical jolting of the oars and the light murmuring of the water".

Unlike Fontane, who stood at the beginning of his literary career when he first discovered the Spree Forest, the

Baroque poet and Lutheran Paul Gerhardt

had long established himself when the aftermath of the Berlin Church Dispute drove him to Lübben, then still part of Saxony. A ten-volume edition of his Lieder had already been published. Fontane would later declare that to him a single stanza from these songs was "worth more than three thousand ministerial edicts".

In 1930, the Nikolai Church of Lübben, in which Gerhardt had held sermon, was named Paul-Gerhardt-Church in his honour. A stone statue in front of the portals of the church commemorates the poet, and his severe preacher's countenance looks down on his successors from the vestry window. Perhaps that is too much of an honour? Once in Lübben, Gerhardt never wrote another line of poetry. And yet, one could easily assume that his Baroque "Depart, my heart, and seek ye joy ..." was inspired by a barge tour through the Spree Forest. ■

The lead-glas portrait of Paul Gerhardt hangs in the vestry of the Lübbenau church that was named after him.

Depart, My Heart

Depart, my heart, and seek ye joy
in what the lord bestows
in this sweet summertime.
Take in the lovely gardens' grace
and behold how for me and you
they have spruced up their charms,
they have spruced up their charms.

The trees are laden with ripe foliage,
the earth covers its dust
under a green dress,
narcissus and tulips deck themselves
out much more beautifully
than Solomon's silk.

The lark rises up into the air,
the dove flies out of its lair
and into the forests.
The highly gifted nightingale
fills and relishes with her tale
mountain, hill, fields and vale.

Myself I can't and don't wish to rest;
God has turned out all to the best,
thus awakening my senses;
I sing along and let my heart pour out
which pleasantly rings
in the Almighty's ear.

Geh aus mein Herz

Geh aus mein Herz und su - che Freud in
die - ser lie - ben Som - mers-zeit an dei - nes Got - tes
Ga - ben. Schau an der schö - nen Gär - ten Zier und
sie - he wie sie mir und dir sich aus - ge- schmük-ket
ha - ben, sich aus - ge - schmük-ket ha - ben.

You can hardly tell that the walls of the tower belonging to Schloss Lübben are several feet thick. During the last years of the monarchy the grand heraldic room in the tower was decorated with the coats-of-arms of the estates of the Niederlausitz. Today the room is used for concerts and lectures.

Bottom: interior of the Schinkel-Kirche in Straupitz.

Previous double spread: the Brandenburg cows had much rather graze the meadows than stay in their barns – as for example these cows near the Schinkel-Kirche of Straupitz.

The Spree Forest festival in Lübben offers an excellent opportunity to admire the elaborate Sorbian costumes. You can also find demonstrations of traditional craftsmanship, as for example the manufacture of ceramics shown here.

Far right: better homes in Lübbenau: although cement housing projects were erected for the coal miners and the old town was increasingly neglected during the 50s and 60s, many of the old half-timbered houses have been preserved.

HEARTY, SOUR AND SPICY

Fishermen, farmers and craftsmen have shaped the Spree Forest for centuries. Accordingly, the local cuisine had to taste good and cost as little as possible. Hearty

home-cooking rather than haute cuisine

Bon appetit: in the Spree Forest every menu features fish in delicious Spree Forest sauce.

was the order of the day, using foodstuffs which could be fished, hunted, slaughtered, milked and harvested locally. A tradition to which the proprietors of the old

Wotschofska inn or the more recent, post-unification restaurant Zum Nuß-baum still adhere. They make their guests especially happy when they present them with the "silly season" dish of sour pickles. These small, crooked delicacies are typical of the Spree Forest. They must be well-seasoned and crunchy, either fresh from the wooden barrel or out of the glass jar with the Spree Forest logo under crossed snake heads. Already in the old days it was known all over the Spree Forest that sour pick-les from Lübben "cleared women's and men's heads". It was also com-mon knowledge that "Kneedel, Leinell and Quark make you strong". Boiled potatoes are called *Kneedel* in this area; served together with onion curd and flax oil, *Kneedel* are a well-represented feature on every menu.

Freshly caught fish is also a must in the Spree Forest. Every cook favors his own special recipe for the light Spree Forest sauce that best accom-panies pike or pike-perch. Very often malt beer and Pilsner are added to the suds which are then refined with flour and sweet and sour cream and spooned in proper style. During the 17th century, art professor Woite enjoyed "delicious

young pike with the even more delicious Spree Forest sauce" at the inn Zum Fröhlichen Hecht in Lehde. He not only invented the name for the inn, founded in 1640, but even implemented a very modern market-

cake irons, *Plinseneisen,* before the eyes of the guests at the restaurant Kaupen No. 6 in Lehde. Perhaps a more difficult dish to get used to is *Gritzwurscht,* a black pudding which is sold right on the ice in

ing strategy by enticing his artist colleagues to visit the Spree Forest through brochures. The artists' paintings, in return, were the ideal means of attracting public attention to the Spree Forest.

As everyone knows that love goes through the stomach, *Hefeplinsen* are probably also a very good source of advertisement for the Spree Forest. The Slavic pancakes are baked on special pan-

winter. A coal grill is mounted on an old-fashioned transport sled and subsequently surrounded by a flock of hungry ice-skaters.

If your digestive system should happen to be slightly overwhelmed by these culinary specialities, you can always rely on a *Kümmel* schnapps from Schlepzig to settle your stomach. Or perhaps you would prefer a sip of Likendeelers Spree Forest bitter? ■

From the fields right into the pickle barrel or jar, or perhaps even better right into the kitchen of the Pohlenz-Schänke restaurant at the southern edge of the Hochwald. Spree Forest specialities are a treat for your taste buds, even when they are consumed in "spirited" form from the bottle.

Inviting, colourful, and folksy: during the Lübbenau barge parade, which takes place every summer as part of the Spree Forest festival, traditional customs can be admired in all their beauty and diversity.

HOW TO BUILD A
SPREE FOREST BARGE

Ready to go: barges in a private harbour (top right). The most important step in barge building is the bending of wooden planks over an open fire.

In spring, when the barges, the most important means of transportation in this region of abundant water, receive a new protective coat of paint, a faint smell of tar wafts through the air. Afterwards, the wood is left to soak in the water, so that all the cracks will close up. Visitors are frequently astounded to find barges that lie half-drowned in the Fliessen for this purpose. Max Petrick from Raddusch knows what he is talking about when he explains that "barges that are taken care of in this way will last at least 30 years. If not, they only last about three years." As a joiner who has just recently retired, Petrick has spent his entire working life building barges. Now his son is continuing the prosperous family business – in the fourth generation. A new joiner who has been trained by

Periodically renewed coats of tar help to preserve the barges, the traditional means of travel.

the master craftsman himself was hired especially for the building of barges.

The flat barges which have no keel are still built according to traditional design – if one disregards the use of circular saws and drilling machines. Petrick explains that the barge builder

himself goes into the forest to handpick the wood from 130-year-old pine trees. Before it can be further processed, the sawed-up wood has to sit for two years. Only then can the boards, which are constantly wetted, develop the right elasticity for the sides of the barge. It takes about six to ten days to manually manufacture one of the curious vehicles that appear so portly, but which can be manoeuvred on the Fliessen with minimal effort. It takes skill, not big muscles, to successfully steer a barge.

"A barge can be no larger than 30 feet long and 6 feet wide",

as Petrick mentions. "The measurements of the sluices don't allow them to be bigger." The floating work of art, including the 13-foot punting pole, the "Rudel", and complete equipment, costs 2,000 to 3,000 pounds.

At the Spree Forest Museum in Lehde, the visitor has an excellent opportunity to inspect barge building techniques and tools. Barges were still built in the museum workshop until 1992. Today it is open to the public.

Petrick and the other three barge builders of the Spree Forest consider the metal and plastic barges which enjoyed a certain amount of popularity for a while a thorn in their sides. The craftsman from Raddusch complains that "they do not belong here". Not because he is a traditionalist, but for aesthetic reasons and because of the unbeatable advantages of the raw material wood:

"A wooden barge simply can't sink."

And Petrick's craft will surely not go down either. The organisers of barge tours have long realised that the millions of visitors to the Spree Forest prefer to be punted through the water labyrinth on wooden barges. Plastic – no thanks ■

Max Petrick from Raddusch and his colleagues belong to the few Spree Forest joiners who continue to master the difficult art of barge building.

The Spree Forest as a winter wonderland: during the cold season time seems to slow down here. As soon as the ice covering the Fliessen is solid enough, the traditional push-sleds are brought out. Large hay stacks, as shown in the background of the large photo, allow the farmers to store hay outside of the barns.

The Spreewald-
museum in Lehde,
with its cabin
farm-houses,
gives impressions
of rural life during
the 18th and 19th
centuries.
The Stallgaleriebau
shown here
belongs to a farm
in Burg which was
transported to the
museum grounds.
Smaller animals
were kept in the
lower part, the
maids' room and
food reserves
shared the top
floor. Baskets,
earthen jugs and
bottles (below)
belonged to the
sparse household
effects.

The elaborate embroideries of the Sorbian costumes show how much love and care is put into their making. Every village has its own embroidery colours and designs.

THE SORBS – A LANGUAGE AND CULTURE

Freshly printed once a week: the "Nowy Casnik" keeps the Sorbian minority of the Lausitz informed about present news and events. There are also historical reports on the past of the Sorbian population.

"A Sorbian paper? I'm afraid we don't carry that. Only German and English papers." This is the answer given to anyone who asks for the weekly *Nowy Casnik* ("New Times") – the Sorbian newsletter that offers eight pages of up-to-date information to the Sorbian minority in the region of Lausitz (Lusatia). Sorbian, or Wendian, hasn't been spoken in the area of the Lower Spree Forest between Leibsch and Lübben for a good 150 years now. Even in Lübbenau, the "gate to the Upper Spree Forest", it is in vain that one cocks the ear for a friendly "Dobry Den", which means "Have a Good Day". Sorbian is a dying language, almost exclusively spoken by older generations.

What immediately catches the eye of the visitor to the Spree Forest, however, are the bilingual village signs. Lübbenau is also Lubnjow, Leipe is Lipje and Burg Borkowy.

The latter is the biggest village in Germany, comprising 34 square miles of dispersed farmlands. Here, but also in Raddusch, Straupitz and of course the big city of Cottbus (Chosebuz), you can still meet Sorbian-speaking descendants of the western Slavic tribes who settled in the region between the sixth and eight centuries AD. Their's was not an easy lot, though, as they had to struggle against Germanic attempts at expanding and germanising territories in Eastern Europe, a process that began in the 9th century and continued up to the National Socialist period, when the Sorbian language was no longer allowed to be taught in German schools.

The GDR, on the contrary, made great efforts to preserve the Sorb heritage. Indeed,

the Sorbian minority has succeeded in keeping its past alive.

The Sorbian spoken in the Spree Forest resembles Polish, whereas the Sorbian spoken in the area of Bautzen (belonging to Saxony) relates more closely to the Czech language. Today there are about 40,000, some

The head-dress of the Lübbenau girls is far less elaborate than the bonnets of the women of Burg.

Eggs painted in a unique Sorbian wax-painting technique are in high demand as souvenirs.

sources even mention 60,000, people who cultivate the Sorbian language and culture. They are supported by the Domowina Association and the Foundation of the Sorbian People. Moreover, the state constitutions of both Brandenburg and Saxony guarantee special rights to the Sorbian population. In school, they are still taught in Sorbian, and there is even a Sorbian high-school in Cottbus. The media organization ORB regularly airs Sorbian shows on its third TV channel – a venue for Sorbian language and culture, which thanks to bilingual transmission is also worth seeing for German-speaking viewers.

And every once in a while the German-Sorbian folk theatre group from Bautzen stops by to present guest performances in Lower Sorbian.

The Sorbian heritage comes alive when the villages celebrate the traditional events of the Zappust carnival, the Stollenreiten across the harvested fields or the "Hahnenrupfen", the plucking of the roosters. During the Hahnenrupfen, a horseback rider must attempt to grasp the head, then the wings of a rooster which has been hung from a raised joist. The winners are then crowned with wreaths by young women in traditional attire. ■

Embroidery has always been a favorite activity of Sorbian women during the long, cold winter nights.

Zur Förderung der öffentlichen Gesundheitspfl wird dringend ersucht, in den Bahnhofsräumen, auf den Bahnsteigen, Treppen und in den Wagen nicht zu spucken.

Previous double spread: afloat in Lehde. Individualists prefer to tour the forest in canoes. The boats can be rented out just about anywhere.

Memorabilia from the Spree Forest narrow-gauge railway at the Burg station. Today you can enjoy a hearty meal surrounded by numerous curiosities, such as old signs and train tickets. Meals are also served in the restored coaches if desired.

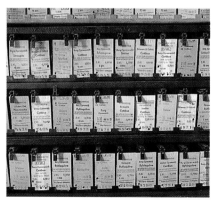

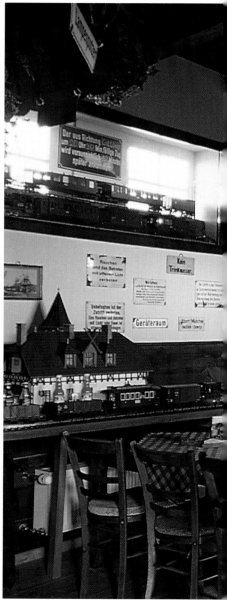

In the waiting room of the former train station beer is brought to the tables by means of a toy railway. Be careful not to spill your drink when the innkeeper sounds the steam whistle!

Old fisherman's house in the district of Kauper, belonging to Burg. Already the early inhabitants savoured pike, perch, tench and carp as fresh-water delicacies.

A tour alongside, on, or across the Fliess at Raddusch (top) or Burg (centre and bottom) guarantees complete calm and relaxation.

Architecture framed by nature: Schloss Vetschau, built in 1540.

Below: the Wendian-German twin churches of Vetschau share the tower and the vestry, the roof of which can be seen in the foreground. The church bears witness to the age-old coexistence of German and Sorbian culture. The German church, inaugurated in 1694, was built wall-to-wall to the Wendian church, which is in dire need of restoration.

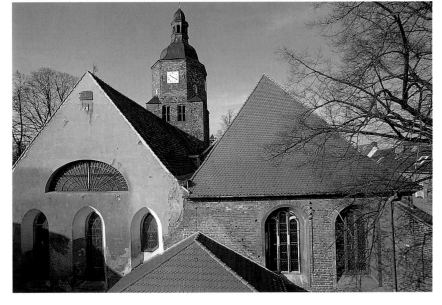

The Spremberger
Turm, 101 feet high,
on Breitscheidplatz
square is a
landmark of Cottbus,
the ancient town
of clothes-makers.
It is not open
to visitors.

Following
double spread:
lignite surface mines
in Welzow–Süd.
As soon as the
excavation bridge
has laid open the
beds of coal,
the fossil fuel can
be dredged from
the earth.

DINOSAURS OF THE MINING INDUSTRY

This is how it's done: an information board at one of the look-out points into the mines of Welzow-Süd.

As if it had escaped from a futurist version of "Jurassic Park": a power shovel in the mines of Welzow-Süd between Cottbus and Schwarze Pumpe.

Behind the last house of Grötsch, a gap of two to three feet yawns in the rusty noise barrier. Here curious visitors can catch a glimpse of the moon-crater landscape of the Jänschwalde surface mines near Cottbus. Only in recent times have the mining grounds been opened to public inspection; in the GDR the state energy reserves were kept top secret. Nowadays, the Lausitz coal mining association, abbreviated as "Laubag", advertises adventure and exploration tours around the mining pits, whose gigantic excavators tower over the grounds like steel dinosaurs.

The heart of Jänschwalde is called F 60. The name derives from the excavation bridge with a length of 2,132 feet (650 meters). According to Laubag, this is the largest mobile machine in the world. Its function is to remove the surface layer on the northside to a depth of about 160 to 200 feet, and to then dump the loose ground on the southside, which has already been stripped of its lignite (brown coal) reserves.

F 60 travels through the mines on 3 miles of shifting tracks, almost touching the border with Poland in the east and cutting its way towards Horno in the north. The inhabitants of Horno are fighting like David against the Laubag-Goliath. They don't want to share the fate of the people of Kausche, who had to leave their homes to make room for the surface mines of Welzow-Süd. They resettled in Neu-Kausche, where they insist they have become quite happy after all.

– about 50% of the entire European lignite reserves.

There is, of course, a drawback. Billions of Deutschmarks are necessary to ecologically regenerate the pock-marked landscape. In areas where the coal has already been removed, a lake landscape surrounded by forests and farmlands has been planned; for example in Lübbenau, where a nature recreation centre is being constructed. A great concern is the water economy of

Laubag extracts tons of coal for the nearby power stations with the help of special "chain-bucket" excavators. This keeps the lights burning in the state of Brandenburg.

Supporters for and against lignite mining have shown little interest in compromising. The fossil fuel, which developed over twenty million years, still offers the economically floundering area of Lausitz about 10,000 much needed jobs. During the GDR there were at least 75,000 jobs to be found. And coal mining guarantees continued productivity of the power stations and briquette factories. The long-term prospects for the labour market and energy economy are quite promising, since another 13 billion tons of the "black gold" still lie dormant in the Lausitz

the Spree Forest. For the coal to be exploited from the mines, the water table has to be lowered considerably. Most of the water extracted here must be pumped back into the Spree River – if not, the Spree Forest would dry up completely. Estimates have shown that it will take at least 20 to 30 years for the water table to reach its previous balance. A new lake landscape will have formed to the south-east of the Spree Forest by then, hopefully providing water with the adequate acidity to attract fish and water plants. And swimmers, of course. ◼

The "black gold" from the Lausitz is also processed into briquettes which feed the tiled stoves that heat many of the old houses.

*Left page:
the old market
square of Cottbus
with its
statue-fountain
lies at the heart
of the city.
In the background
the tower of
St. Nikolai high
church overlooks
the square.*

*The remnants
of the city ramparts
bear witness to a
turbulent past.
The Wieckhaus (left)
is attached to the
ramparts as snuggly
as a swallow's
nest to the wall.*

*Theatre, opera
and ballet have
found a home here:
front view of
the Cottbus
Staatstheater.*

59

COTTBUS AND AN ECCENTRIC PRINCE

Poet, dandy and world-traveller: garden architect Hermann Prince of Pückler-Muskau as portrayed on a wooden engraving based on a photograph from 1863.

There are plenty of things for the people of Cottbus to be proud about. But more than anything else they take pride in their Staatstheater. As the people from Cologne love their cathedral, the people in Cottbus relish the impressive Art Nouveau theatre built by architect Bernhard Sehring. After only 16 months of construction, the theatre was opened with the staging of Lessing's *Minna von Barnhelm* on October 1, 1908. Today the building, after undergoing extensive restoration in the middle of the 80s, is known to house the most important theatre in

the state of Brandenburg – not least thanks to its magnificent ensemble.

The high regard in which art and culture are held in the birth-place of painter Carl Blechen (1798 – 1840) is surely also due to brilliant Prince Hermann von Pückler-Muskau (1785 – 1871). This man, who designed the park in Potsdam-Babelsberg for German Emperor William I, was not only an excellent architect of gardens, but also one of the most eccentric personalities of the previous century. Goethe praised him as a writer, and women flocked to him like moths to a flame. When the world-traveller and gourmet

Tamed wildcats: there are many fascinating details to discover inside and around the Art Nouveau building of the Staatstheater, and not only on stage.

lifted off to a balloon ride as early as 1816, the Berliners could hardly believe their eyes. They must have been even more shocked to find Pückler-Muskau riding up to Cafe Kranzler in a carriage drawn by two stags. He was trying to impress his bride.

The Prince spent barrels of money.

Most of it went to his garden projects, one of which he realised in Muskau. Unfortunately, the Prince was forced to sell the park in 1845 for two million Thalers to financially salvage his estate. He later built another landscape garden in Branitz near

green Prince. Not only your eyes, but also your taste buds will find plenty of stimulation during a visit to the park when Cottbus cooks get together and serve multi-course menus which follow the Prince's meticulous books on the pleasures of the table. If you enjoyed the meal, you may pay your respects to the Prince at the Tumulus, the earthen pyramid in Branitz Park where Pückler-Muskau was laid to rest.

Prince Pückler-Muskau is often mistaken as the inventor of the ice-cream flavour named after him. This

Drinks can be bought in the upper foyer of the theatre during intermission. Gourmet and bon vivant Prince Pückler-Muskau would have done just that. He was laid to rest alongside the remains of his wife Lucie in the Tumulus of Branitz Park, which lies in the middle of the Pyramidensee (sea of pyramids) of Branitz Park.

Cottbus. The Branitz Park was an essential feature of the Cottbus Bundesgartenschau (national garden show) in 1995. Indeed, the Branitz castle and the many winding paths and walkways surrounding it still seem to breathe the spirit of the

is not so. It was rather a confectioner from Cottbus with a mind for business who began to market his ice-cream creation under the aristocratic name. The gourmet and bon vivant Prince must have enjoyed the delicious dessert as well. ∎

Branitzer Park

angelegt von Fürst Pückler im Jahr 1846

"This is certain that, if I succeed in creating an aesthetic nature, this will be my masterpiece": Hermann Prince Pückler–Muskau achieved the goal he had set for himself with Park Branitz. Left centre: a terracotta relief from the wall of the pleasure grounds in front of Schloss Branitz, on the bottom a detail from the music chamber of the Baroque castle.

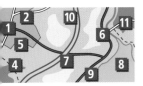

AT A GLANCE

1 Bahnhof Burg

Today the former station of the Spree Forest narrow-gauge railway (in operation from 1898 to 1970) houses **a restaurant offering Spree Forest specialities.** There are also numerous **memorabilia collected from railway-men** on display, including restored coaches. *(Burg; Am Bahnhof 1, tel. +49-(0)3 56 03-8 42)*

2 Lignite Surface Mines

The communities of Grötsch and Briesnig offer **look-outs** into the mining grounds of Jänschwalde. The northern Cottbus mines can be viewed from Bärenbrück Heigths or the Cottbus district of Schlichow. The Laubag information centre on the grounds of the Cottbus Bundesgartenschau stages changing exhibits on the subject of energy resources and power generation. *(Laubag-Öffentlichkeitsarbeit; Senftenberg, Knappenstraße 1, tel. +49-(0)35 73-78 30 50)*

This sign shows how to get to the Lübbenau train station.

3 Haus für Mensch und Natur

Excellent **permanent exhibit on the Spree Forest biosphere reserve,** emphasizing man's impact on nature and culture landscapes. *(Lübbenau, Schulstraße 9: open Mon-Fri 9 a.m. – 4 p.m.; additional hours from April – Oct.: Sat, Sun, and holidays 10 a.m. – 5 p.m.; for guided tours call +49-(0)35 42-8 92 10)*

4 Hochwald

The two-hour **barge tour** doesn't really allow the tourist to savour the atmosphere of this fascinating region. It is best to embark on a longer tour that includes the Hochwald. The barges depart from either Burg or Lübbenau.

5 Naturlehrpfad Lübbenau-Lehde

A **nature study path** (ca. $1/2$ hour) which teaches about the **plant world of the Spree Forest.** The birch-lined continuation of the hiking path runs parallel to the water.

6 Schinkel-Kirche

In 1832 this **Classicist building** with twin towers was erected by Berlin master builder Karl Friedrich Schinkel. The church is only open to the public during mass - just like most of the Spree Forest churches. *(Straupitz, tel. +49-(0)3 54 75-1 67 71; mass Sun 10 a.m. Tours directly follow mass; additional visiting hours May – Oct. Mon – Wed and Fri 5 p.m.)*

10 **Staatstheater Cottbus**
The unique **Art Nouveau building** from 1908 is home to a **magnificent theatre ensemble.** *(Cottbus, Am Schillerplatz 1. For information and tickets call +49-(0)3 55-7 82 41 40)*

Left:
inside view of the Agrarhistorisches Museum (museum of agricultural history) in Schlepzig.

7 **Schloss und Park Branitz**
Delve into the **world of eccentric Prince Pückler-Muskau,** who created a garden paradise here.
(Cottbus, Zum Kavaliershaus 11; tel. +49-(0)3 55-75 15 21. Open Nov – March Tue-Sun 10 a.m. – 12 p.m. and 12.30 – 5 p.m.; April-Oct. until 6 p.m.)

8 **Schlossturm Lübben**
Medieval ramification tower with walls 8 feet thick. The estates of the Niederlausitz used to meet in the **heraldic room** of the tower.
(Lübben, Ernst-von-Houwald-Damm 14; tel. +49-(0)35 46-41 31. Open Tue – Sun 10 a.m. – 5 p.m.)

9 **Spreewaldmuseum Lehde**
Three farms dating from the previous century in the centre of the lagoon village" illustrate the traditional wood building technique of the region. There are also demonstrations of rural Sorbian life and culture. (Lehde, tel. +49-(0)35 42-24 72. Open April 1 – Sept. 15 daily from 10 a.m. – 6 p.m.; Sept. 16 – Oct. 31 from 10 a.m. – 5 p.m.)

Additional Information
Tourist Information Spreewald: Lindenstraße 1, 03226 Raddusch; tel. +49-(0)3 54 33-7 22 99, fax +49-(0)3 54 33- 7 22 28; internet: http://spreewald.imedia.de. Fremdenverkehrsbüro **Cottbus:** Karl-Marx-Straße 68, 03044 Cottbus, tel. +49-(0)3 55-2 42 54. Fremdenverkehrsamt **Burg:** Am Hafen 1, 03096 Burg; tel. +49-(0)3 56 03-4 17. Fremdenverkehrsverband **Lübben and surroundings:** Lindenstraße 14, 15907 Lübben; tel. +49-(0)35 46-30 90. Fremdenverkehrsverein **Lübbenau and surroundings:** Ehm-Welk-Straße 15, 03222 Lübbenau; tel. +49-(0)35 42-36 68. **Natur- und Heimatverein Unterer Spreewald:** *Dorfstraße 26, 15910 Schlepzig; tel. +49-(0)3 54 72-2 25.*

Top:
sign-board of the Cottbus Apotheken-museum (pharmacy museum).

Left:
map of the hiking paths around Lübben.

1 **10**

These numbers (1 – 10) refer to positions marked on the map on the inside front and back covers

CHRONOLOGICAL TABLE

The coat-of-arms of the city of Lübbenau.

400 000 – 20 000 BC

Glacier masses plane the surface of the land during three ice ages and form the moraine landscape at the southern border of the Spree Forest. Glacial waters form the bed of the Berlin-Baruth River. The low incline of the land forces the Spree River to fan out into many smaller streams and Fliessen to get past the rubble and alluvial sands.

C. 8000 BC First traces of stone age settlements.

C. 1200 BC During the Bronze and Iron Ages the first large villages develop.

7th to 8th centuries AD

Western Slavic tribes settle in the area. Ramparts dating from this time can still be found in the Lausitz.

10th century AD Germanic tribes begin to settle in the east.

Fliess near Raddusch.

1150 Lübben is first mentioned in documents.

1156 Cottbus is first mentioned in documents.

1304 Brandenburg purchases the region of Lausitz from the Wettiner dynasty.

1621 The counts of Lynar, originally from Italy, purchase Lübbenau. Today their descendants run Schloss Lübbenau as a hotel.

1618 – 48 During the Thirty Years' War the Lausitz is completely ravaged and the population is forced to seek refuge in the labyrinthian Spree Forest.

1748 Manufacture of linen begins in Burg.

1846 Prince Hermann von Pückler-Muskau plans the construction of Park Branitz around the Baroque castle, built around 1772.

Middle of the 19th century

The first lignite surface mines come into existence in the Lausitz.

1866 The railway connection from Berlin to Lübbenau and Cottbus is opened.

1912 The Domowina is founded as the parent organisation of Sorbian associations.

1937 The Domowina, sermons and school classes in the Sorbian language are banned.

1945 Towards the end of the war Cottbus and Lübben are almost completely destroyed.

1950 – 1974 New dammed-up lakes on the Upper Spree and flood canals to the north and south of the Spree River prevent further floods and droughts in

the Spree Forest. These measures, together with the newly erected power stations in Lübbenau and Vetschau and the dramatic increase in population also take their toll on the ecological balance of the Spree Forest.

1989/90 After unification the tourism industry is restructured according to the principles of the free market system. The reduction of jobs in the coal mines leads to a sharp increase in unemployment rates.

1995 The Bundesgartenschau (annual national garden show) takes place in Cottbus.

1996 The Lübbenau and Vetschau power stations are turned off and destroyed.

1997 Plans to resettle the community of Horno for the benefit of the Jänschwalde coal mines lead to heated discussions in the state parliament. Long talks will precede any final decision.

Left:
the Spreewald-museum

The Bismarck Tower in Burg

Following double spread: Schloss Branitz was commissioned by August Heinrich Count of Pückler according to plans by an unknown building master. In the foreground lie the pleasure grounds and Pergola.

The oldest photo shop in Burg/the Spree Forest.

SPREEWALD

179
Ahrensdorf

96
Teupitz
Halbe

Baruth
13

Unterspreewald

Schlepzig

Charlotten-
felde
115
Golssen
Spree

Lübben
8
Biosphären

102
Dahme
Luckau
Lübbenau
3 5 9
Lehde
Raddusch

87
Niederl

Hohenbucko
96
Calau

Finster-
walde

13

1 Bahnhof Burg
(Spreewald-Spezialitätenrestaurant)

2 Aussichtspunkte für den
Braunkohletagebau

3 Haus für Mensch und Natur
(Biosphärenreservat-Ausstellung)

4 Naturschutzgebiet Hochwald

5 Naturlehrpfad Lübbenau - Lehde

6 Schinkel-Kirche

7 Schloss und Park Branitz

8 Mittelalterlicher Wehrturm

9 Spreewaldmuseum

10 Jugendstiltheater

Stürtz-REGIO.
Practical, packed with
illustrations – great souvenirs.
Stürtz Verlag GmbH,
Beethovenstraße 5,
97080 Würzburg, Germany